DEBT TO THE BONE-EATING SNOTFLOWER

Debt to the
Bone-Eating Snotflower

SARAH LINDSAY

COPPER CANYON PRESS
Port Townsend, Washington

Cover art: Klari Reis, *Petri Dish Painting*. Mixed media in Petri dish, 3.5"
diameter. www.klariart.com

Copper Canyon Press is in residence at Fort Worden State Park in Port
Townsend, Washington, under the auspices of Centrum. Centrum is a
gathering place for artists and creative thinkers from around the world,
students of all ages and backgrounds, and audiences seeking extraordinary
cultural enrichment.

LIBRARY OF CONGRESS CATALOGING-IN-PUBLICATION DATA

Lindsay, Sarah, 1958–
[Poems. Selections]
Debt to the bone-eating snotflower / Sarah Lindsay.
   pages   cm
Includes bibliographical references.
ISBN 978-1-55659-446-5 (pbk.: alk. paper)
I. Title.
PS3562.I51192A6 2013
811'.54—dc23

2013022001

9 8 7 6 5 4 3 2 FIRST PRINTING

COPPER CANYON PRESS
Post Office Box 271
Port Townsend, Washington 98368
www.coppercanyonpress.org

ACKNOWLEDGMENTS

Grateful acknowledgment is made to the following publications, in which these poems first appeared, some in slightly different form:

Alhambra Poetry Calendar 2013: "The Casimir Effect"

...and love... (Jacar Press): "Side by Side"

Cave Wall: "Milk-Stone," "Stradivarius Secrets"

The Georgia Review: "Last Will"

Guernica: "In Angangueo"

Gulf Coast: "Rhubarb Wine" (and in *Alhambra Poetry Calendar 2011*), "Sweet Potato God"

Illumen: "Planet Anhedonia" (and in *The 2011 Rhysling Anthology: The Best Science Fiction, Fantasy and Horror Poetry of 2010*), "Ships of Gold"

Narrative: "Iphigenia in Aulis," "Jade Elephant," "Plumbing Goes Everywhere"

New Ohio Review: "Aunt Lydia Tries to Explain the Many Worlds Theory," "Carnivorous Sponges of the Antarctic Ocean," "Radium"

The New York Times: "The Driver"

O. Henry: "She Touches My Hand"

Orion: "Coastal Nevada Zoo and Animal Studies Program," "Red Fish, Blue Fish"

Parnassus: "Adaptive Behavior" (and in *Poetry Daily*), "'And his trails do not fade,'" "How I Was Born," "Lithographs," "Only One Known"

Poetry: "Hollow Boom Soft Chime: The Thai Elephant Orchestra" (and in *The Best American Poetry 2012*), "Shanidar, Now Iraq," "Without Warning"

Poetry Northwest: "Aunt Lydia Attempts a Few Observations," "Debt to the Bone-Eating Snotflower," "The Leviathan of Parsonstown," "Origin" (Pushcart Prize)

Prime Number: "Speaking of the Octopus," "The Whiteness of the Breastbone of a Goose," "Wind-Whittled"

roger: "The Common Octopus," "Fish in the Trees," "His Courtship"

The Sound of Poets Cooking (Jacar Press): "Where Dido Dwells"

The Styles: "Jericho Worms"

The author wishes to thank all manner of people and some animals, but will limit herself in print to Michael Wiegers and the staff of Copper Canyon, David Caligiuri for copy-editing perspicacity, Herb Leibowitz for scientific encouragement, Stephen Corey for editing from Tanzania, Mark Smith-Soto and Valerie Nieman for tea and critique, Jeff Klahn and Elisabeth Swain for Darwin Day, Gertrude Burke for the actual jade elephant, Sam Gaines for the Einstein action figure, Cousin Bobby for telling about the catechism, the string quartet for zinnias and pie, her co-workers for consenting to days off, and her family and Mary for more help than she can say. She also salutes the Admiral.

To Chris, Ginny, and Roger, who remember Eotippus,
junkyard barrettes, and a lot of blueberries

CONTENTS

PART 1

Rhubarb Wine

PART 2

Octopus and Others

PART 4

Trails

DEBT TO THE BONE-EATING SNOTFLOWER

Rhubarb Wine

WITHOUT WARNING

Elizabeth Bishop leaned on a table, it cracked,
both fell to the floor. A gesture
gone sadly awry. This was close to fact
and quickly became symbolic, bound to occur
in Florida, where she was surrounded
by rotting abundance and greedy insects.
One moment a laughing smile, a graceful hand
alighting on solid furniture,
a casual shift of weight,
the next, undignified splayed legs.
The shell of the table
proved to be stuffed with termite eggs.
True, it was a fall from no great height—
merely the height of herself,
and although the hollowed-out table failed,
at least the floor held,
though probably infested by termites as well,
and possibly built on a latent sinkhole,
how can you tell?
And how could she, smiling and easy,
arm moving without forethought and permission,
have forgotten fear, apparently
let go of a hard-learned lesson?
Enter a room as though it is strange.
What you recognize may have changed,
or may change without warning.
Trees fall in hurricanes

and on windless mornings,
breaching houses where people you knew
have vanished or died or stopped loving you.
She regained her feet, already composed,
brushing dust from an elbow. There would be a bruise,
but it would remind her that *words are full of holes;*
flung hard, like paper they fly sideways.
And a call to joy—a landscape, a face—
may, though scarcely moving, perhaps by not moving, go
in one breath from heartening to ominous,
proving to children who need more proof
that we don't know what we know.

RADIUM

His gifts to her were theory, patience,
equilibrium, and a pile of dirt—
industrial waste. He loved to watch his wife
aglow with determination, pursuing
discovery of a hidden element, past uranium,
by the light of her hunger. "I should
like it to have a beautiful color," he said.
He would buy her boots to wipe at the Sorbonne.

Heated, she leaned over a boiling vat,
stirring her dirt reduction, hour on hour.
She looked like any skinny hausfrau
bent to her bubbling sauerkraut.
She looked like the first woman who would be
awarded a Nobel Prize, as well as
the first to fall to her knees before
a hill of brown dust shot through with pine needles
and press her filled hands to her face.

She boiled her tons of pitchblende down
to a scraping of radium nearly the size
of their baby's smallest fingernail—just the white.
Proof of its existence, and hers.
It permeated their clothes, their papers,
peeled their fingers,
entered their marrow and slowly burned.

He mildly alluded to rheumatism.
He stroked her radioactive hair
with a radioactive hand.

Colorless, shining radium darkened
in contact with air. Chemically
much like calcium, it could stream
like calcium through her brain cells
in her later years alone
and make memories glow in the dark:
illegal schooling, unheated rooms,
subsistence on tea and chocolate. Lying
with her husband for a few hours' sleep,
cracked hands and weakened legs entwined,
united gaze resting on the vial
of radium salts they kept beside them every night
for the lovely light it shed.

IPHIGENIA IN AULIS

With leftover horses and pompous haste,
obedient to my father the king,
we crossed to the harbor town, my mother and I,
in separate veils of dust,
acting out the pretext of our summons—
that I was to wed spear-wielding Achilles,
despoiler of cities and women.

But the streets were jammed with restive men
enlisted for the Trojan fight,
and still as far away from Troy
as last month when they arrived.
A goddess was offended;
her altar required my virgin blood
before the slack sails would lift again.

Now shining Achilles speaks,
so he believes, in my defense.
I see my mother's teeth
as though she smiles.
The brazen hero dares my father's wrath
by calling for my life,
not asking my preference.

My mother will not comprehend.
For many years, she has relied
on a fortifying anger. Lately

I have glimpsed its quick blade
as she begins to guess that I intend
never to sink
to that source of strength.

I have traveled from one place to another,
yet they feel the same.
What is so precious about this outdoor room,
land that swallows us even before we die,
walls drenched in monotonous light,
great stones dragged, small ones kicked here and there,
ceiling of dread sky?

I know our ships fumble along the coast,
yet sailors who return
pour tales from thirsty throats
of lives barely snatched from the sea.
Then a ship sets out again,
and those watch who are left behind
till it becomes a small delicate toy.

I have seen the rotten sponge
a keel becomes
when it stays in a harbor too long.
I know my own mind.
I choose the four ascending notes of the sacrifice

over a wandering tune
that has no end.

I will be remembered
with more beauty than was mine
once I am ceremonially gone,
and will no longer be the toy
of a mother's wrath, a father's mustered men,
nor any wind,
capricious or divine.

MILK-STONE

The space our town fills is a thin one
between the haunted hill and the sea.
We climb the slope when we must, especially
women seeking help with our bodies'
tides of too much, too little.
Under thornbushes, beside tilted rocks,
we scratch the uneven dirt, where
scraps of smashed pottery work their way out
like splinters of bone from a broken arm,
and sometimes we find ourselves milk-stones:
sea-green, sea-blue, milk-green, milk-blue,
carved on their four long sides
with spirals and suns, ax blades and trees.
Mine shows a bent arm with five sharp fingers.
It hangs on yarn between my breasts
to draw the milk forward, so my son will once
know the feeling of having enough.
He pulls hard, he makes me thirsty,
but my lips keep patting together and sucking
on baby, baby, baby talk.
Today he's a year old.
We'll take him to the harbor and throw him in.
If he floats back to us we know he will grow
and be strong and make the sea feed him.
If he sinks I must turn the string
till the stone lies between my shoulder blades,
to draw the milk back in.

THE MUMMY WALKS

Only two mushrooms to eat this morning,
sprung from the top of my right foot,
pale slender stalks with drooping lids.
They scarcely had weight when I laid them in my mouth
where my tongue used to be
and gnashed my teeth.

For years I could count on waking to plenty,
my ribs a field of oyster caps,
puffballs tenderly bunched in my armpits.
Long morels covered with twisted mouths
were my crown, my collar, my ears;
I never went hungry.

Then for a season I bore a strange fungus,
a pure burnt mineral black, absorbing
every available grain of light
and falling apart like charcoal at a touch.
I ate it, since it fed on me,
and yet I lost ground.

Where I used to live, rings of gilled umbrellas
materialized in the grass wherever they chose.
So, shrunken in my bandages, hollow-legged,
I pace wet gutters in daylight traffic,
holding my remnants wide to the breeze
for any spores that will have me.

HOW I WAS BORN

I think I began like the pig's heart
beating in its tray, or the anemic rats.
A protein mesh was my mother,
and the zipper teeth of my DNA
came from powdered sugarcane.

When I was just one hundred fifty cells,
they plucked one out and carried it off
for a stranger with defective marrow.
"This won't hurt," they said.

I filled the space in anyhow.
I grew, I got the trick of breathing,
fed from an IV.
Learned to drink from a bottle.
Who knows if my origins explain

my fear of needles, my cravings for salty food,
enclosed warm spaces, pale young men with leukemia.
Full grown, I often suck my thumb.
That way I know it's mine.

COASTAL NEVADA ZOO AND ANIMAL
STUDIES PROGRAM

Here at the Coastal Nevada Zoo,
the goal of our program is the yield
of animals viable under the new conditions.
It's a work in progress.
As you see in the Africa Pavilion,
we have sustainable herds of gray zebras
and short-necked giraffes. A few mini-elephants
lived past infancy, but we lost them.
We had one vegetarian lion;
it wasn't my idea to place him
in the former petting zoo.
Next morning we had bones and sated sheep.

The aquarium may be phased out for lack of funds.
Our placid sharks would stop swimming and drown;
the reef our corals built is handsome
but microscopic. We've kept a few
of the long-legged penguins that won't go near the water
and one blue whale that's bigger than a breadbox.
The North American Pavilion is closed.
The leprosy-resistant armadillos
died of flu, the bears refuse to move.
The Rabbit House is a big draw—
people love to watch them fight. This way, please,
and don't forget your masks and umbrellas.
Too many pigeons here, shoving and stretching

for spilled kibble, water, we can't get rid of them.
I've tried. That burbling noise they make,
their imbecile round red eyes, the droppings,
the fleas, and they're fat but always hungry,
same as they ever were.

PLANET ANHEDONIA

Its orbit shrugs.
Its default landscape lacks a horizon,
thanks to the jellied atmosphere.
No abundance, no open water,
no silence—a snoring wind endlessly shifts
loose ends this way and that,
and sulfurous burps erupt from heaps of cells
that lately evolved enough to itch
but still have nothing to scratch with.

But over there, to the north of those hummocks,
a few of those itchy cellular clumps
have developed a preference for the smell
their mucus emits in the four-day damp season,
every six years or so. And a few
have begun to recognize a sensation
related to being not dormant, in fact
related to replication. They almost feel eager.
Their troubles are only beginning.

And over there, to the east of that gully,
a few other heaps have added another
behavior to itching and burping and doing nothing:
they pay attention, biochemically,
to what their neighbors are doing, and sometimes

they shake in response, it's like itching but different—
they're tickled. Therefore
they too will survive.
Like it or not.

ONLY ONE KNOWN

From each of the storage drawers in the Leiden museum
where specimens lie in their lonely multitudes, a dry
and not unpleasant smell arises, of
"never mind, not so interesting after all" —
permission to shut it again.
One drawer holds the only known example
of the otherwise unremarkable bird
christened Sharpe's rail. The only one known
to have been seen, alive or dead,
by anyone. Bought from a dealer in Amsterdam
in the 1860s, a furled double handful
of drab black feathers, dull dark beak,
origin unknown. Another bastard
of promiscuous chance, who populates land and sea.
Perhaps, like the laughing owl, it had
a taste for accordion music;
or, like the Rodrigues solitaire,
it shed tears when captured.
Perhaps in its fruitless search for a mate
it mingled with the pink-headed ducks
in the semisacred swamps of the sacred Ganges,
or braved the thin air of the foothills
with the Himalayan mountain quail.
Its feathers, in life, may not have been this color.
Its cry was raucous; no, its voice was sweet.
Its flesh tasted rancid, or so delicious
that predators gave it no peace

and left none for us: Behold the sole fowl
untasted by man. Or it could have
come from one of those happy islands
on which sailing ships conferred
lavish gifts of rats, until
the land wore a seething surface of fur;
pink toes bent and scrambled over
eggshells long licked clean.
The visitor who obtained this singularity—
someone in love with travel and short of money—
claimed that it puzzled the natives. They spoke of
the *nua,* "bird that follows the hunter,"
the *oihi,* meaning "bird that goes dressed for the festival days,"
the *muneawahi,* or "tasty bird," and many more;
for this one, he said, they had no name.
But who is disposed to believe these tales,
unsupported as they are
by the little stuffed labeled fumigated body?
Sharpe's rail is just another in the orderly ranks
of flightless wings with motionless feathers,
claws without grip, breasts without pulse,
eye sockets plugged with white cotton wool
to maintain each face's final expression:
Alas, I am discovered.

JADE ELEPHANT

Where elephants wore green cloaks of plenty
and walked in green shoes, new with every step,
shoveling green food into their mouths,
smoke rises. Farmers are hungry, their children hungry,
the soil of their old farms starved;
they need new fields. They burn more forest.
And where the rotting carcasses of elephants
lie flattening on trampled grass,
smoke rises. Poachers are hungry, their children hungry,
but two rangers, not so well fed either,
took away the prize. They tend with oil
tusks in a jumble bound with flames.
No ivory thrones permitted from this waste,
no combs or roses or tiny pendant monkeys.
Clots of smoke rise from the tusks and mingle
with mountains of smoke from the trees,
and when a later rain falls into
Poland, Wyoming, New Zealand or Guatemala,
Siberia, British Columbia, Japan,
or closer, in Yunnan, Tibet or Burma,
with a few dark drops for Italy,
it seeps into veins of stone. Ornamental nephrite,
green and brown. Precious jadeite,
its color determined by iron content,
some clouds shedding more blood than others.
Here come hunters. Maybe they're hungry,
maybe they're young bulls always in musth,

unable to stop their weeping and craving,
tearing down more trees than they eat,
gouging out hillsides, fouling the water.
They throw aside most of the stones they find
and take the pretty ones home. Some chunks
give rise in the hands of carvers who hold them
an itch eased only by the making of an elephant—
uplifted trunk, for luck (which is hope
compact enough to be transferred),
broad head with ungainly wings of ears,
four thick legs like trees holding up
a small slow green brown planet.

HOLLOW BOOM SOFT CHIME:
THE THAI ELEPHANT ORCHESTRA

A sound of far-off thunder from instruments
ten feet away: drums, a log,
a gong of salvage metal. Chimes
of little Issan bells, pipes in a row, sometimes
a querulous harmonica.
Inside the elephant orchestra's audience,
bubbles form, of shame and joy, and burst.
Did elephants look so sad and wise,
a tourist thinks, her camera cold in her pocket,
before we came to say they look sad and wise?
Did mastodons have merry, unwrinkled faces?
Hollow boom soft chime, stamp of a padded foot,
tingle of renaat, rattle of angklung.
This music pauses sometimes, but does not end.

Prathida gently strokes the bells with a mallet.
Poong and his mahout regard the gong.
Paitoon sways before two drums,
bumping them, keeping time with her switching tail.
Sales of recordings help pay for their thin enclosure
of trampled grass. They have never lived free.
Beside a dry African river
their wild brother lies, a punctured balloon,
torn nerves trailing from the stumps of his tusks.
Hollow boom soft chime, scuff of a broad foot,
sometimes, rarely, a blatting elephant voice.

They seldom attend the instruments
without being led to them, but, once they've begun,
often refuse to stop playing.

WHERE DIDO DWELLS

Retired five years ago today,
Dido the circus elephant still knows
under which sycamore she buried
commands she might thenceforth fail to obey.
Strolling amid the flickering trees,
she avoids its shade.

Where she dwells, mastodons gloomily ate
"Indiana brains," Osage oranges,
when there was nothing else. The bitter fruit
thus propagated Dido spurns,
plucking blackberries instead with lazy finesse
from between their thorns.

RHUBARB WINE

Was it anyone's favorite? Or simply
the time-honored choice of settlers far from luxury,
"better than nothing"? Color of sauerkraut juice,
or late November daylight. And it wasn't the flavor,
wrung from stems of inedible leaves,
that warmed the heart, but the promise
in ruined sugar that lightens the blood
so one's head, almost weightless for an hour,
doesn't pain its shoulders. Anything they could ferment
was a prize from the grudging garden
where rhubarb laid shadows
on loops of okra pods and vines
that might yield a squash or turnip's worth of bounty,
where the bright things—pretty wings and petals
and spotted caps—were almost always poison.

THE WHITENESS OF THE BREASTBONE
OF A GOOSE

The whiteness of the breastbone of a goose
infallibly tells how thick the snow will lie
while there is yet time to prepare.

The goose is killed for its secret. No matter,
its down and flesh will cover the children's ribs.

Of course for the heavy hand of winter
the farmers assess as well the behavior of squirrels,
the timing of birds of passage, the thickness
of onion skins. Anything to shake loose
a hint of what comes next, what to do,

though Jakob with his yellow eyes
and Fred with his rosy spectacles
will come to different conclusions,
and Karl, rubbing his face with filthy hands,
can never agree with his brothers.

White that conforms to ground and seals it like sleep.
White hummocked over wagons and fences.
White that blinds a man to the way home
six freezing steps from his door.

They bend to read the feathered wreck,
their heart's blood chanting *My roof, my fields,*
my cow, my wandering son,

thick with riddles—they wield a blade
to gouge out mere foreknowledge,

splitting a seaworthy sky-gray vessel
that might have sailed on,
appearing on the dark river white itself,
if not for snow.

SHIPS OF GOLD

The people who lived there grew used to having
a man in the mountain,
as they grew used to lacking the others
crushed in the tunnel that trapped him.
They all took turns, with Ettor and Binia in charge,
carrying food to him—what they could spare,
and a few scraps more. And to keep him
from too much silence
back there in the dark,
schoolchildren recited their lessons
where he could hear them, reported prizes
and played flute duets, but softly, softly,
nothing to stir the uncertain rock.
Men brought him news, and women gossip,
with how much overlap he didn't say.
But no more talk of rescue after
the terrible last attempt.
Everyone knew the routine: Just half the daylight
went with you beyond the entrance, and most of that
was lost where the tunnel bent. At the rockfall,
push the sack you brought
far enough through the crooked opening
so he could reach it,
although he couldn't see you;
reach in with a clean jar
and take the used one.
Soap on Sunday, and extra water.

Routine, as well, the greeting at the fissure,
"Still there?" which they began to use
with each other, too,
till it wasn't a bad joke, just habit, like thinking
there will be five at the table instead of four.

The last lamp has long burned out
in the swollen rubble, where further explosions
may yet be biding their time.
His ears have stopped ringing.
He no longer wakes himself
shouting. The feral dogs
or whatever they were have given up
sniffing and scratching at the slot
that tells day from night, that lets in
air and food and sounds of the world,
blankets, a cushion
whose color he doesn't know.
Sometimes, after the students leave,
their times-tables make a white parade
around his head, or he spends a while
piecing together their list of kings.
He might try to herd into line, mutter-singing,
the words of a song he thought he knew.
Or think about the orange they brought him,
and dwell without much hope
on the chance of another.

Most often, though, he speaks with his comrades
packed in a ton of ore.
Remarkable things they've learned in there.
Stories of travelers, dragons and beautiful women,
three sisters, a river, a ring, white horses,
wars and dooms and ships of gold.
That is, until four days ago. Or five.
Could they have gone? He feels the fractured
wall with his fingers. Without him? He pulls
his lobes to widen his ears.

Binia came up the slope with her bundles,
the usual cheese and bread, and an orange,
faintly proud she hadn't peeled it
and eaten a piece on the way. She entered
the rock mouth, then stopped
to make out what she heard:
his voice, repeating at intervals,
not speaking to her, and
a little too loud, "Still there?"

THE LEVIATHAN OF PARSONSTOWN

On Earth, for threescore years and ten,
it was the widest eye—
the Leviathan of Parsonstown,
a telescope of forty tons,
its stone house open on two sides,
weighing down the emerald green
in Irish fog and mist and fog and rain—
a giant cannon created to swallow light
and trained on cloudy skies.

In the new foundry's hottest fires
bogs' worth of peat were burned
to make the metal mirror shine,
a flawless hero's shield
that focused blobs of light beyond Orion
into blue-white spirals, signs
of artful order. But in the ground
lay blighted potato crops (were stars malign?),
and soon the famished men.

Its mirror was later melted down
for war's unbounded needs,
leaving its blinded barrel mouth to say,
Although one night in ten I could
see what was mine to see,

could fetch down from between the clouds
perfectly visible spiral nebulae
and knowledge craved by some as food,
it did, it seems, no good.

PART 2

Octopus and Others

CARNIVOROUS SPONGES OF THE ANTARCTIC OCEAN

We are adequately nourished or dead.
We are near the optimum temperature or dead.
Currents feed us. Shadows pass between us
and the light when there is light.
We are clustered in a suitable place or dead.

Faceless, gourd-shaped animals clamped
to the floor of a frigid sea,
they wait for the sway of water to introduce a sea louse, a
    worm, an ostracod,
then snag it with spiny teeth, or toothlike spines.
Sponge-flesh grows slowly
around the prey impaled.

Our family is repeated self.
Our house is columns of water.
Our spectrum of color is dark and less dark,
our music, water against itself,
continuous fizz and percussion. We are
enveloped in movement or dead.
Firm in our grip or dead.

The populations of the abyss
have no business with the charismatic
megafauna fathoms higher—orca, penguin, albatross—
nor even with ice. Occasionally

a castle berg gores a ship
whose wallowing body, releasing plumes of oil,
settles where it will.

We are washed in brine but not preserved.
We do not shiver or complain, admire
or even see ourselves, cry out
or grimace with our many shallow mouths,
pockets in which we keep nothing.
We hold to life as though it is dear to us.

We neglect to give thanks
to the tender pink plantlike oceangoing worm
called *Osedax mucofloris,*
which has no concept of us,
no sense of being recently discovered,
no name for herself, or thoughts on our name for her—
in English, "bone-eating snotflower."
But without her (and the him she keeps,
for his lifetime, in her body), every
seashore would be barricaded
by skeletons of whales. The tides
would rattle.
         Blushing in the shallows
where hagfish undress a recently stilled leviathan,
the snotflower strokes a fresh white surface,
presses against it,
eases her animal roots through, into
a scapula, a rib, perhaps
the vestigial pelvis, and eats or drinks
or otherwise absorbs the structure,
and when she leaves, it's gone.

In her useful diligence she resembles
the worms that stir our fields from below,
the worms and cousins of worms that tend our woods
so logs and carcasses haven't piled up
higher than the pine-tops. And so

we can go on gardening, hiking,
throwing Frisbees on the beach, ignoring
the ugly ones, the specialists,
minute, nocturnal or hidden from light,
the smudge, the slime, the particles
in their modest trillions
that shield us from excess
while ignoring us too—
                          and further kindly
keep their slurps and snips and whisks
and hooverings from evolving beyond the sky,
where they might tidy away dark matter and leave us
sleepless under unbroken sheets of stars.

ORIGIN

The first cell felt no call to divide.
Fed on abundant salts and sun,
still thin, it simply spread,
rocking on water, clinging to stone,
a film of obliging strength.
Its endoplasmic reticulum
was a thing of incomparable curvaceous length;
its nucleus, Golgi apparatus, RNA
magnificent. With no incidence
of loneliness, inner conflict, or deceit,
no predator or prey,
it had little to do but thrive,
draw back from any sharp heat
or bitterness, and change its pastel
colors in a kind of song.
We are descendants of the second cell.

LITHOGRAPHS

the Solnhofen limestone

Prepare the solution.
A shallow sea
lies warmly over coral reefs,
placid as anything on this choleric planet.
Waters penned by coral
grow saltier; oxygen fades. There
nothing lives but blue bacteria
and mariners in tiny shells.

Prepare the plates.
In these bitter, calm lagoons
the breathless mud is soft, composed
of limestone's finest grind:
husks of foraminifera, coral,
calcium once shaped by life,
settling speck by speck in layers
hardly ever stirred.

Prepare the specimen.
A minor flurry as the floor
receives an organism: drifting limp,
or fallen if winged or dropped if not,
an error. In the anoxic brine
it lies perfectly still, sooner or later,
where no teeth or germs will hasten decay,
where calcium powder
sifts accurately upon it.

Print of a single feather
from a time of pterodactyls.
Subtle mark of a jelly.
Form of a horseshoe crab, and the last
few meters of its trail. Traced wing
of a dragonfly, persistent
jaws of a turtle. Crinoid, ammonite, wasp,
a puppy-sized dinosaur, *Compsognathus,*
with undigested lizard in its belly.

Limestone was quarried for pyramids,
cathedrals, roads, paper, toothpaste,
soil conditioner, supplement
for poultry, source
of calcium in our bread.
What fossils were split and crushed
and ground? A *Compsognathus*
reproduced in such detail
we could have read its thoughts?
Its neurons, like ours, flooded with calcium ions
in the process of rendering memories.
Its brain, like ours,
was the center of everything.

SPEAKING OF THE OCTOPUS

A swirl of pickled silk,
        saltwater slipknot
                stronger than she seems,
        adept at attach- and detachment.
Apparently aimless bouquet of boneless limbs,
        she does not have a shape,
                but about
        forty thousand three hundred twenty,
with a tendency
        when not in pursuit
                to gesture in several directions at once,
        expert in self-contradiction, adept
at obscuring her wits
        with a talent for drifting,
                propensity to hold still, stay still,
        her thin skin taking the color of what she dwells on—
she does excellent impressions of water and stone.
        Her face a pair of voracious eyes
                and a fierce mouth hid
        in the single pit of her arms. She can fit
through keyholes, open the lids
        of glass boxes and climb in or out, but prefers
                the amniotic wrap of the sea;
        daily she reads its endless blue page, or
down where there's darkness, thoroughly
        fingers the Braille of a coral reef.
                Quieter than eight snakes, her unfurled

                anemone of flesh
trails her sac of a head until
                she finds something desirable, chases it,
                        clasps it in arms
                that give it a hundred cold kisses—or, if
she is too deeply moved,
                makes a decoy self of ink
                        and dissolves behind it.

IN ABEYANCE: BDELLOID ROTIFER

Slight thickening of liquid,
faint hindrance of light,
a microscopic
plump nozzle shape,
I purify water. Fish meal, dead algae,
flecks of rot I devour,
spinning the whiskers around my mouth.

Unlike a virus,
I seek no host.
I modify only myself,
and that slowly.
Reproduce only myself, always female—
I am my descendant;
I have inherited
endurance.

The ice of a night or an age
hardens on me. Or heat strikes,
and shrinking water deserts me.
Desiccated, I fall open.
Thawed or watered, I form again,
enclosing any genes within reach
from detritus
sloughed at this puddled crossroads.

Therefore I bear, along with countless
scraps of trash, instructions for gifts
I cannot use:
bite of a worm lizard,
beads of a Gila monster,
probing tongue of an armadillo,
silky fur, bright plumage, knees,
a hyoid bone for speech, stirrup
and anvil bones for hearing...

Granted enough of the pattern, I might
have wings, or teeth, blood circulation,
sacs of deadly venom, sleep with dreams.
The social order of ants
lies dormant in me
as I mill the water, solitary.

Somehow I maintain the precepts
for my simple stomach,
the grip of my posterior toes,
the arrangement of my cilia.
Someday, I might acquire
enough of a new idea to express it—
from grass, opacity,
from a centipede, speed,
from a spider, limbs and weapons,
from archaic fungi, ability

to secrete a mighty elixir.
Someday, a sense
of eons and alterations.

I see no lightning,
hear no thunder,
but with rain I awake.
I may have rested a century here
or a day—
same scissor-snip of dark
to the sleeper, same
blink back to awareness
for the fifteen cells of my brain,
the body unfurling refreshed
around its old genes and any they lay with.
Who might I be now?

.

BEACHED

Carrying the water I saved today
in the leaky cup of my hands,
I approach Earth,
beached on her belly
but stirring slightly
in a miserable wind.
As high on one side as I can reach
I let my pittance spill
down the cracked blue skin,
careful of her blowhole,
and I think her squint eye's moon
rolls to see more,
but a hurricane clouds the pupil,
ringed with smoke on fire.

RED FISH, BLUE FISH

The river slowed as its mountains wore down to hills,
it aged from clear to ginger to brown,
it acquired more shade and shallows.
Its changes were easy for fish to learn
in their milt and eggs that retold their story: *silver fish,*
with a blue shine while it lives,
tail twice as long as the head.
Later, for various reasons, *silver-stippled fish,*
blue shine on its back and gold below,
and the beasts that came to the river's edge
were no longer tall as the trees, and the trees that fell
and moored in the water had strangely tender,
splayed leaves. The flies whipstitching the surface
grew slightly bitter, pink flowers made seasonal journeys,
microscopic spikes in the fish eggs murmured
of possible alterations, but there was no hurry.

A stain of light spread over the valley;
tar and sewage marbled the water.
In a single year piles of stone arose in the current
with arching shadows; in one year a wall of stone
interrupted everything. Then from pipes upstream
gushed color; the river ran red a week,
ran blue a day; fish rose from a dream of yellow
to sudden white. Some rocked in the weeds,
some swam in tight circles, some set off upstream
and never came back, some turned up their bellies.

Hobby anglers that hauled a few,
twisting, into the air hadn't been there long enough
to know that the sullen glaze
on the eyes of their apple-green catch
(maybe purple next week)
was one of the newest inventions in the river.

THE ARMS OF A MARVELOUS SQUID

"Let not your heart be troubled," the wise man said,
"for love is stronger than you know."
I was sixteen, seeking lessons in rainbow posters,
love was stronger than I knew. So was fear.
So was sorrow that hauls a heart's bellrope
again and again. So were the bonds
in a drop of water; so was the force of gravity
leading the drop from eye to mouth
or pulling a car with bad brakes downhill
or abetting a body stood on a chair
with a rope around its neck.
So was the force of life in microscopic creatures
deep in solid Antarctic lakes,
or boiled in acid on the Pacific floor,
or duking it out between sickness and health
in a human intestine. And the life
in the devious roots of dandelions,
an elephant's trunk, or a flea's hind legs.
Stronger than I knew was the desire sometimes
to move quietly through harmless days,
eating from a plate, buying stamps or a toothbrush.
Which was more remarkable,
the breadth and depth of my ignorance,
or the strength in the arms of a marvelous squid
that hung in my vision, uncurled as if
about to dissolve, then whipped one length
around my wrist, preventing me

from running away, preventing me
from rising to breathe,
reminding me of love?

THE COMMON OCTOPUS

The octopus has no bones,
the octopus has no voice.
Her mouth is in her armpit,
her body in her head.
She scarcely has a face.
Her eyes are purple squares
in domes with fleshy lids.
She spurts a purple cloud
and safe behind it flies.

She can be a tassel,
she can be a web.
Her hide is wondrous thin,
transparent at the tips.
Her arms are many many,
more fluid than a flame
and lined with sucking cups.
Wet she crawls through fire
or holes as small as dimes.

Color of the ocean floor,
color of the beach
or wherever else she lies.
What I cannot breathe she breathes,
where I cannot go she goes.
Her curling makes me shiver

when I should be moved to praise.
The octopus has no bones,
the octopus has no voice.

CEPHALOPOD AND STAR AND SEA

My right hand is a starfish,
with rough skin, an ability
to anchor itself that looks like stubbornness,
radial symmetry—equal, opposing digits,
like contradictory beliefs—
and a mouth in its palm. What it desires
it changes—keeps in a pitiless grip
and absorbs. If I lose a finger,
it simply grows back.

My left is an octopus,
changeable, malleable, graceful and clever.
Its fingers twine and twirl apart
like thoughts that tangle
but never make trustworthy knots.
It's able to creep through keyholes, wield small implements,
shiver its colors to blend with any surface,
seize eight things at once, then leave them
under a small dark cloud.

They were not happy together at the piano;
they like the cello, the left one sidling
up and down ebony while the right one
governs a rod of command.
They have learned to applaud, they consent
to wash each other, but when they clasp,

either or both may go white at the knuckles,
red at the tips. They do agree
that they sail a cantankerous ocean,

its weather skittish, currents shifty,
coral reefs cracked and mended.
Excitable cuttlefish relay itches and cravings,
awash at times in oil spills,
sugar spills. Not to mention
the sac of heavenly blue afloat in my head,
trailing long wrinkled stinging nerves
down my spine. Not to mention
the bullheaded whale in my chest.

JERICHO WORMS

Out of this rupture,
out of its boiling lesions,
gouts of hot sulfur rise,
laborious smoke,
through groaning plates
of seawater dense as lead

Out of this rupture, bounty
for the Jericho worms
(*Tevnia jerichonana*)
unpleating themselves
to reach the heat

Bounty for the bacteria
(*Beggiatoa*)
that feed on hydrogen sulfide
as if it were light

Paradise for the giant tube worms
(*Riftia pachyptila*),
the scarlet-crested
four-foot-long cigarettes
swooning over the vents,
paradise for the squat violas
of pale brachyuran crabs

Out of this rupture,
this ruinous split,
whose sulfur uncoils
in my guts and my throat
and the roots of my brain,
without sun, without blessing,
hunger springs up,
hunger resumes its work

ISOLATED OCTOPUS

Expanse of water underwater,
goldshot with conciliatory light
whipped in by a storm now spent;
smooth blue solid, featureless, except
an octopus, strange to these conditions,
explores with questioning tips.
No stone no shell no coral rasp or skin to suck
with its cups or teeth to evade,
no shape to relieve its eyes;
the octopus presses its mouth to nothing but water.

Abruptly it rises—or is it sinking,
or twirling sideways, multiple ripple
against a unison heave?
It pauses and sags, breathless, cool.
What it does now resembles waiting,
if waiting can take place without
apparent time to pass.
A loose skein of suspended flesh:
What color is it, undisguised?
What shape, lacking crevice or prey?
The octopus lifts or lowers one arm, touches its face.

Will it remain red-violet? Turn blue-green?
Will it sing like a whale but with eightfold signing,
shine like a street of neon, spin till it flies?

Or will it refine its imitation of water
so neither water nor mimic
knows the difference?

WHALE FEATHERS

They sing, they soar, the whales of our time,
whales of the tropical shallows, the streams
and rivers, the courtyard ponds.
Stone records say there were giants in the seas,
but grudgingly supported, and no more.
Much as the mouse outlived the titanothere,
tiny whales and whales the size of chickens
perch on white twigs of coral, pipe shrill melodies,
pluck up tube worms from cracks
with one neat turn of the head,
or flit through cloudy fathoms
snagging luminous particles one by one.
Much as lizards in shabby plumage
filled a kingdom bereft of tyrannosaurs,
these timid, swift creatures have sprouted
a specialized fur like penguin feathers:
most are brown or gray, but some wear
iridescent amethyst, ruby, silver, trailing
scarves and plumes of musical bubbles.
Little Sargassos of sodden down
form in their molting seasons.
You can keep in your basement aquarium an echo
of beasts large enough to be taken for islands,
to snap the ribs of a ship, to swallow
a man and vomit up his implausible story.
You can ply with cracker crumbs a puff
whose ancestor, Leviathan,

divided the surface with its brow
while its open jaw scraped the ocean floor.
You may cup a whale briefly in your palm,
stroke its back with one finger,
feel its heart beating like wings, and marvel:
oh the precious, the comprehensible world.

Lifting, extending one half-curled arm,
the luminous squid
gently touches her camera's housing;
her breath stiffens in her lungs.
He is three thousand feet below the ship
and the wraith he makes on her video screen.
For this she sailed,
for this she housed lenses
in a cylinder depth won't crush,
endowed with a steady red light
the blue-sighted creatures down there won't see
and a dead fish clamped on for bait.
With long observation
of cool lights alive in the dark,
with remote-controlled imitations of phosphorescence,
she has learned to say *Come here, come look*
in Jellyfish and Shrimp,
has attracted giant six-gilled sharks,
and now here he is,
seven-foot, glowing, camera-shy
Taningia danae;
cluster of powerful question marks,
ripple and flash of blue lights.
He saw *food* first, but then the signal
of a receptive female
with a charming foreign accent,
and he wants to make for her

a superb collection of smooth objects,
present to her lumps of richest carrion,
wrap and not quite crush her in his arms,
smothering just for a moment
her exotic shade of blue.
She wants to watch
his ballet under tons of pressure per inch
for the rest of his life, write down
everything about him, know
how cold and firm his flesh is,
how quick his mind, how strong his tensile limbs,
and, when his skin lights like a meteor shower,
what it says.
But the cylinder is unresponsive to him. He dims.
It babble-flashes. In the last moment
she shouts at his naked eye.

ADAPTIVE BEHAVIOR

Five miles deep,
on the Japan Trench floor,
the forecast is the same today
as for the last million years:
near freezing, cave-black,
five tons of pressure per square inch.
Slow rain of flesh.
Snailfish ask nothing more.
Their plump head-bodies are pale
with dark eyes, reports
the submersible peering
through portals of solid sapphire.
Energetically, gracefully,
they congregate over a meal of shrimp,
waving their ribbon tails.
Snailfish bear large eggs,
deal carefully with their young,
move swiftly in the dark,
in an ocean of pressure—and here
the observers, so easily
drowned or crushed,
thought to find only
feeble, half-paralyzed creatures.
Snailfish move as if joyous,
never pine, fear no grief;
they are strong,
like *Staphylococcus* bacteria tried

for generations by hospital protocols,
strong like earthworms
in old mines who swallow
copper, lead, and arsenic,
yet thrive, excreting
milder poisons.
A snailfish ripples
through Pacific depths,
an earthworm tunnels under England,
and neither bears an enormous brain
that must be fed,
a hearthfire demanding
every tree for miles.
Such brains belong
to the ones who invented
a camera that can plumb the sea
and return, and the ones
who poured the metal
and mined the stone, the ones
who mow their lawns,
wear shoes that hurt,
deafen themselves with music;
the ones with bad backs,
bad knees, terrible eyesight,
who stay up late,
speed on highways,
don't eat their vegetables,

sometimes sit on one side of a bed,
too sad to pull on socks, and sometimes
fall in love
like mangoes hitting the ground;
the ones who scrounged for grants
and skipped having kids
so they could be seasick over the trench
where hypothetical
solitary, anemic beings
listlessly lived—and who leaned
toward their video evidence
of vigorous fish
and made noises of pure delight.

PART 3

Cosmic Turtles

AUNT LYDIA ATTEMPTS A FEW OBSERVATIONS

I suppose you've heard
of the theoretical cat,
trapped in a box,
that is both alive and dead
until someone lifts the lid
and then it's not.
Though study has increased my uncertainty,
it appears
that a particle (or cat)
is where it is only because,
and when, we *see* where it is.
(And as we settle
its location, our chance
of measuring its momentum
must vanish.
Physics may sound
more plausible in Danish.)
Would pre-observation potential
or observed definition
better suit a quantum node?
And, if aware of its condition,
might it consider
the influential observer its god?
Can we detect what it prefers
before we interfere?

Drat. Again I make animal shapes
of conceptual blobs. Well, so be it,
that's how this brain works. Perhaps our job
is not to panic
because we coexist with quarks
on a small, peculiar planet,
but to name the beings in boxes,
lift the lids, draw
our deity's attention,
so divine sight
acts as defining intervention.
It surveys all cats
with inhuman comprehension,
yet possibly It designed, through us, a sense
in which It may experience
suspense.

MAGNITUDE: AUNT LYDIA DOES STRETCHING EXERCISES

A soft sweet cheese they make for daily bread,
and in the vat of milk and rennet set an egg,
to tell them when it's done. While they're
feeding the chickens or sowing corn, the whey
congeals in streaks and superstring curls.
Rifts develop, curdy lumps,
and gases congregate in spirals;
the smell grows desirably rank as elements
thicken into earths and metals,
and when our unhatched robin-blue planet
sinks, this batch will be ready.

Or maybe enough dark matter exists
for turning out firmer cheese,
a dark dark marbled Swiss with black holes
and delicious veins of stardust forming
from windborne impurities, along one of which
our Earth is a fleck of blue mold.
Maybe they wrap it in burlap, so
the rim of this universe bluntly prints
a coarse fabric weave on the next one.

Think of the milch cow they keep, its size,
the heat of its flanks, the weight of its hooves,
think of the one who comes to milk her,
whistling square roots, perhaps, or wave functions,

think of the breadth of space in the swinging pail.
And think how you've nonetheless fit the whole barn,
for a minute at least, in your head.

AUNT LYDIA AND THE COSMIC TURTLES

Three or four elephants hold up the world
in Chinese and Indian myth, their flat feet
planted on the back of a very large turtle.
The modern tale, as Aunt Lydia understands it,
says everything, from the merest idea of a nanospeck
to the milling gaggle of galaxies, is endowed
with natural exigence. In the so-called
higher forms it may be called desire and more easily thwarted,
but each kind persists in the way of its kind:
photons fly at the speed of light,
electrons flit in strict atomic spheres,
magnetic fields align and iron obeys them,
water expands when it freezes.
Cytosine binds with guanine and guanine only,
rotifers whip their fraction of pond,
Parajuresania lies in soft sediment,
eggs hatch, mostly, and baby sea turtles
paddle on sand directly into the sea—
or move toward the sea as long as they can move.
Butterflies, penguins, whales with gallant smiles
migrate along long lines that seem straight
but follow the planet's curve, as planets curve
around cycling swirling stars—
although at this moment, in fact, off Maui,
striped and black and bright yellow fish
are nibbling algae and itch from the neck and shell
of a green sea turtle that lounges in comfort

and closes its eyes, declining to behave
mythically. Nevertheless, when Aunt Lydia
shakes from her own mind thoughts of comfort
and nature programs and love and chocolate pie
and peers within her soul as best she can,
she sees a vindication of the old story:
Her faith, sometimes an egg, or a heap of ash, sometimes
for full milliseconds on end a fragrant blossom,
but often an ordinary serving platter, is borne up
by ancient creatures, dignified and silly-looking,
their peculiar features developed to suit
another time, their tree-trunk legs
set firm on the back of a turtle, older still,
with that resolute seagoing look in its eye—
and as far as Aunt Lydia's nearsighted eyes can see
it is indeed turtles all the way down.

IF GOD MADE JAM

If God made jam the jars wouldn't necessarily glow
like Christmas lights or the new home of seventy fireflies,
the berries wouldn't have to be so divine
they dribbled rainbows and healed the sick,
each pip released a *Gloria* when it
cracked between your teeth,
and God's jam would never refuse to touch earthly bread—

Aunt Lydia has worked out this much
since Cousin Bobby told her about a comma
he skipped long ago while learning his catechism.
Now, on a rainy morning, spared the news
that lay in her grass and is too wet to read,
she's flexed her stiff hands and found them able
to slice the bread baked by a friend
and twist the lid from a royal-red jar,
and with the first crusty, raspberry bite
she's ready to affirm God does make jam.
It still counts if people figure among
the instruments that have been put to use,
and Bobby catechized wasn't wrong
when he pictured a deity, willing to work in the kitchen,
who made preserves and redeemed us.

AUNT LYDIA PRACTICES LOVING
KOMODO DRAGONS

If I'm meant to love people, I should love everyone.
What kind of tide can an ocean bestow
if it picks and chooses the rocks it's willing to touch?
But oh, those hard ones: him, and them,
and you-know-who—gah. What was she *thinking?*
Hm. Time for an exercise.
I'll start with Komodo dragons.

First, *love:* not meaning lips and limbs,
mush, or even understanding.
This love is not a melting of self,
a softened apprehension of the other.
The loved one need not meet my gaze,
acknowledge my presence,
approve or know of me.

Now I turn my welcoming
and accurate regard upon a Komodo dragon.
A viscous string of drool hangs from its jaw,
sparkling in dry-season sun.
Its slit eyes follow the dying cow
whose swollen hock it gnashed two weeks ago.
A dragon's chronically oozing gums
nourish with blood the germs that poison its bite.
(I'll try to love germs later.)
Let my soul embrace the creature that waddles forward

to rip the skin from its fallen victim's belly.
Perhaps if I close my eyes.

Bless the creature, it does what it must.
Of course, it may be a mother, it may have
commandeered for its eggs a mound of dust
laboriously amassed by a scrub fowl—
that's easy to love, a shamefaced bird
that spends its courtship
building a hill with its toes, for the sake of
hatching hunchbacked babies one at a time...
Too easy. Back to the terrible lizard,
whose father broke some other male's leg in combat
for the chance to pin down a struggling mate,
like his fathers before him.

Perhaps if I think of the cute little babies—
well, little at least, unaware
of the mother's fierceness on their behalf.
She's gone when they hatch.
The first thing out of the eggshell's crack
is the flicking forked white tongue,
tasting for danger. It's easy to die on Komodo.
Not enough rain. No plenty. No ease.
And who wants to die? Wait—yes, here it is:
love for the lizards, even the dark adults,

the lame, the broken-legged, the breakers of legs,
with their graceless gait and their stinking breath,
who seek warmth in the morning and shadows at noon,
who grapple unquestioningly with their lousy life.

Meanwhile, their island is far from me;
they sneer at no one, flaunt no opinions.
Tomorrow with the newspaper spread before me,
I'll unclench my fists and try with people again.

AUNT LYDIA CONTEMPLATES LIFE, ART, AND PETRI DISHES

In between experiments, Sir Alexander Fleming
amused himself by growing microorganisms
of different colors and textures so arranged
in petri dishes that they (or he) made pictures.
A *Mother and Child* in tender shades of mold.
My House: recognizable, but highly toxic.
One might have guessed someone with a hobby like that
would discover penicillin—by accident.
What would that be like, to be living paint?
We wouldn't know, would we? Suppose
the grapple and angst, honks and candles
of human carryings-on from the hairy beginning
have been planned and pruned and coaxed along
in a planetary dish turned toward the sun
by some Flemingial artist, to achieve a pleasing effect.
That some dabbler not in color, but in
four-dimensional hues of tension, irony, and surprise,
has set and kept us going just
to form a likeness—say, an Annunciation,
Gabriel proclaiming something too large
for us to grasp, in a voice too angelic
for us to recognize.
The invention of the wheel might be
the tip of one of the angel's feathers;
the collapse of the Ottoman Empire, the weft at one end
of his drapery (and why he wore plaid we're not to know);

the gift of five cows to a co-op in Zimbabwe,
the gold speck that brightens Mary's brow.
I mean of course the equivalent of a gold speck
to a macroFleming who watches us through black holes,
or whose eyes are black holes known and unknown, or
who cannot be said to have eyes.

Would that fate be so terrible?
If everything we do or try to do
limns an omniFleming's Georgia O'Keeffe magnolia
or Marvin Cone shadowed staircase, what of it?
We could be glad to be part of art,
wish mildly that we could see it, and keep doing.
Oh, of course, *free will,* that nut
that's all uncrackable shell. Don't worry;
any Flemingacious gardener knows
free will is one of the colors our species refracts,
and positions us with that in mind,
wouldn't you think? We might be surprised
to see our position in the design,
which could turn out to be chiefly a showcase
for cacao trees, or nematodes, or penicillium molds,
while we're perhaps the comic relief,
or a purply-rose transition in one corner,
or a shimmer, as when, for a passage in Wagner,
the string sections sacrifice hours of precision fingering
just to be a blur under the horns.

We should practice glad humility,
and tell ourselves it's good for the health:
I'm sky behind Grant Wood's pitchfork!
I'm a second violin in *The Flying Dutchman*! I'm beige!

And the masterwork that we in our smallness
partly compose, meanwhile, could be
one letter of a sampler being
embroidered on a void with helium and hydrogen,
for practice. Or one stitch
in a still-expanding quilt where our universe
is the newest crazy patch.

AUNT LYDIA'S METAPHYSICS, WITH OCTOPUS

Sprung from a body that can't hold it any longer, the soul
rises, past need or pain. Never mind
monotonous bliss or harps or wings,
we won't know till we go, I was told
when Daddy died. But it rises.
I thought of soul-balloons on strings,
floating up all over the world.
I was too young or sad to care
that souls released in China and Des Moines
would fly in pretty much opposite directions,
or one soul turned loose at midnight and one at noon.
Could *up* be everywhere? Later
I thought of an octopus and its ink,
how it sheds an octo-blot decoy and escapes —
so while we, the bereaved, tended a fading image,
the true self flew away gracefully, safe,
swiftly, with many arms. That would be fine —
what bothered me most was that souls might dissolve
    without skin.
Then I read that two particles, once connected,
are bound ever after — it's hard to explain,
like everything in modern physics,
but if one happens to spin,
the other spins correspondingly,
though a universe lies between.
It's not a reaction; they still behave as one.

So, taking my science personally,
I can believe a thing might be diluted,
be immeasurably, invisibly thin,
and still be him.

AUNT LYDIA TRIES TO EXPLAIN THE MANY WORLDS THEORY

At every decisive moment—and every one is decisive—
the universe frays.
Though naturally it seems wide enough
to us to be exclusive,
it's merely the latest bit of the thread
we're following through a maze,
and whereas its time seems linear to us,
every point explodes,
blossoming like fireworks, or fuzz.
It's only a theory, "many worlds," but if it's true,
in some worlds you're driving a red convertible,
in some you play French horn—
brilliantly, in one.
In quite a lot you don't even have
the bother of existence.
Elsewhere you're the only son,
elsewhere identical twins.
Perhaps in twenty-two of the many,
you and Paul Newman are best friends,
and talk about life and love and fast cars.
In three hundred fifty-four you have his autograph.
In nine he has yours.
Multiple yous might be right now in your favorite spot,
rubbing your favorite beast behind the ears,
thinking, "This is perfect contentment," although of course
inevitably in some other wheres

your selves feel quite the reverse.
True, the you here can't visit that world
where humans live without back pain,
or the two or three without mosquitoes, or mold,
but then, you don't have to sample the versions
lacking in mangoes, or memory, or rain.
In any case, so to speak, this world alone
is stocked with enough to keep most of us entertained—
supernovas, living fossils, nephews and nieces,
fillips like two species of worm
that feed upon whales' bones—
but what a twenty-first-century sort of comfort to believe
in infinite secret alternatives.
Add the many worlds together
and you have the time you need.
The lost are found, the lost are alive
and the living whole, diseases are cured,
missteps corrected, untried paths tried;
you take in strays, make bread.
No limit to the things that are.
Here you still walk the wire,
but put your hand just a second or two ahead
and you'd feel it split so many times
it's soft, like fuzz, like fur.

SWEET POTATO GOD

"A table, a chair, a bowl of fruit, and a violin,"
said the frizzly physicist,
"what else does a man need to be happy?"
A source of warmth. Chocolate cake.
And what about books? what about sheet music?
Some of us don't have the knack of traveling light.
Asked to outfit a paradise,
I'd begin with breads and books and dogs
and lie awake thinking, What if I start to miss maple trees
and their spinny seeds? wet garden hoses?
the smell of frying onions?
and in the end, I'd take the world along.
What would you leave out? Gravity?
No more broken hips or skinned knees
and look at us, we're flying—but
our hearts are weaker, our bones dissolving.
Mosquitoes? The bats are faint with hunger.
Feed them your favorite butterflies,
or the mango, unpollinated, will go extinct.
I'm not finished packing, I'm adding the zinnias
Allan brought in a jelly jar.
Bowed by Hurricane Isabel,
their stems curved out of the mud in loops and elbows,
raising pink purple red orange Einstein heads.
I want a chunk of iolite, a mineral
colorless or blue, depending

on how you view it; a piece of honeycomb,
likewise plain or intricate; a paring knife;
rosin for the violin bow.
And a sweet potato god—a plain rock
the size of a healthy tuber,
with dents for a face. At the proper time,
in fertile soil, Old Polynesians
buried him with the planting,
buried a prayer for the growing season, acknowledgment
that more than what we need is necessary.

AUNT LYDIA TAKES OUT THE GARBAGE

In a weak moment, one of many,
right on the verge of throwing away
a column my sister tore from the paper and sent me,
I looked at the other side.
ago Tribune, it said. *MPO.*
veloped by music and
orges its world-famous,
using a mysterious
centuries old
Below that, a face in shadow, a short sleeve edging
the tender dent in an outstretched arm.
So that piece of newsprint was strange and I had to keep it;
that's why my desk is such a mess.
I know it's wretchedly inefficient,
this What if it's trying to tell me something,
this What if the dirt I'm standing on
is sown with pre-Clovis arrowheads, hiddenite crystals,
ants in a beautifully burrowed nest
like a hollow mold for seven-foot strands of kelp?
What if beneath my feet—oh dear,
I've walked out in my socks again—
I know it's an extravagant habit of mind.
But who wants to stare at the bland white side
of a honeycomb all her life when an overhead view
of hexagonal cells could explain so much?
Or to stuff an unexamined sack in the can

when fascinating trash could be inside? This twilight is lovely,
and I don't mean to sound ungrateful
for Orion, Cassiopeia, and Galileo, but may I
turn over a scrap of sky?

AUNT LYDIA'S JUNK DRAWER ANTICIPATES THE DAY OF JUDGMENT

Behold, I will tell you a mystery.
When the last day comes, and the trumpet sounds,
the catchall drawers shall all fly open
and their contents shall be changed.
Probably the drawers themselves, as well,
maybe even the linty dust in their corners.
The rusty pin, the nutless bolt,
one battery left in a package that held four,
the small box full of cotton,
they shall rise incorruptible,
radiant with their essential beauty,
and, best of all, useful and put to use.

Mind you, that's no reason to make them wait.
Scruffy wire twists, blackened rubber bands,
off-kilter paper clips, even that quaint old relic,
string, bring them forth, set them to work,
let them feel needed. Wet down the gray stones
you picked up in who knows what river,
watch them remember their loveliness.

Imagine the wonders of the supposed Day of Wrath
when the least of these shall be judged and found wanting,
only to be restored: glove to lost glove,
the fingers mended; pipe cleaners straightened;
smooth shoelaces displaying manicured tips.

Plenty of room for all in a land where,
astride the bronze lion pacing with all four legs,
the three-inch plastic baby doll reveals her glory,
splendor of her bald head, majesty of her short striped dress,
power of her bright blue eyes
no longer forced to close when she lies down.

And from the back of the drawer
where cringing knuckles pushed it,
snarled in a hank of raffia for thirty years,
the leaden floral-arrangement frog will rise shining,
its rows of rigid needles, no longer dangerous
when nothing can be harmed,
perfectly holding imperishable flowers.
Or perhaps it was meant to be or desired in truth
to be a real frog, a pulse in a membrane
of scarlet and olive, or a spiny sea urchin
bussing the seafloor, or a sharp burst of gamma rays.
May those of us who wonder find out
whether it's given a choice in that final moment
or gladly fulfills a destiny beyond choice
when its turn comes to meet the Being, the God, the One
whose names we will know, whose ways we might understand,
who was in the drawer too, all along.

Trails

"AND HIS TRAILS DO NOT FADE"

A memex is a device in which an individual stores all his books, records, and communications.... It is an enlarged intimate supplement to his memory.

VANNEVAR BUSH, INVENTOR, 1945

Unsmiling Venus, queen and captive
of the imperial hallway, overlooks
the shifting, multilingually noisy crowd
saluting with upraised camera phones.
No photo shows the paint once bright on her lips and eyes,
the heavy gold chain she wore, the golden apple
held in her gaze and her lost left hand.
She keeps no scrapbook. Will we remember
the onion smell of the sweaty boy beside us,
the assertive elbow of the girl
who pushed through to pose at the marble knees,
remember how sore your feet? The roof of my mouth
still tender from the raking crust
of a café sandwich?

How many wielders of cameras
remember Vannevar Bush? His "memex"
was meant to preserve every sight, every thought,
every path through the forest of information:
The man of his future, tiny camera strapped to his forehead,
inaudibly clicking, taking copious notes,
"builds a trail of his interest
through the maze of materials available to him.
And his trails do not fade."
Picture him hauling a little red wagon

stacked to the sky with microfilm
that frees his mind for exploration,
trailed by his stenographer and his librarian,
his records swelling like mushrooms in rain.

The mythic, long-desired third eye
installed above his spectacles
sees merely what the first two see.
The memex files, no matter how thickly
scrawled with arrows, won't reproduce
the action of neurons packed in a skull
like the tender capsules of juice in an orange segment,
nerve impulses spreading sideways as well as end to end,
so a dream of snakes touches off a molecular theory;
a certain angle of sun through trees means
love, or the exquisite sting of a wasp on the thumb's web;
frying pork chops evoke
her hands approaching my face,
slowly, skin smelling of onion and orange peel.

How did he see, through his theoretical camera,
compulsive record-keeping as liberation?
But in Paris we too scribbled as we walked,
paused for snapshots whose glowing aura, conferred by
    our presence,
only we can perceive. Winged Victory

stood as an eight-inch replica
by the door to the basement stairs
for forty-three years in my parents' house.
Here she soars in gray radiance above us,
figurehead of ships long dissolved.
Breasting the spray of salt minutes
and gusts of travelers' exhalations,
she spreads her plaster wing for flight
and her mended marble wing with its iron brace.

THE PROFLIGATE SON

At his mother's funeral, October brightness
buttered the run-down Appalachians
in all directions and fell on the church front steps
condensed in ladybugs. Standing by a pillar
before the service, he approved of the scarlet blundering dot
on the breast of a cousin's black dress.

They closed the lid on her secret love and anger,
or at least on a lot of jewelry. Let her keep it;
she lost two sons, two husbands, a lung, her memory.
The bite of her grave in the churchyard looks too big
for what was left. But then, this hill and all the mountains
keep giving themselves to the valleys anyway.

Back on the stone steps, full in the sun,
goodbye minister, goodbye cousin, goodbye cousin, goodbye,
    goodbye,
red shells landed on everything, ladybugs
snagged on scarves, spotted the columns, fell underfoot to
    be crushed
and reddened the puddles of yesterday's rain. He saw how well
he was taught to be wasteful as though he had enough.

FISH IN THE TREES

Tambora volcano, 1815

After the explosion
it was not safe to move for some time.
Wisely or not, they lay still.
Relations between many things were altered:
The ceiling was too close to the floor;
fire went anywhere but the hearth.
Pieces of ground propped up trees,
which held fish in their branches,
while birds moved slowly in the water near shore.
A bowl might cut like a blade;
a plate might scorch worse than the stove,
a bunch of flowers burn hotter than either.
Spaces meant to be empty were filled—
doorways, pipes, skies, nostrils.
Others accustomed to fullness were swept clean.

The horizon line has changed, they agreed,
exhausted, surrounded by wrack.
The sun is a different color.

Time enough later to count what was left,
move things to their former places,
careful not to set their feet
where anything might break.
Remember quiet evenings when
he sharpened a knife, she cooked a chicken.
Night after night they lay together

awkwardly, and touched without stroking,
because their skin was gone,
and their bodies were charcoal.

SIDE BY SIDE

He shuts off the kitchen light and leaves
two plates to dry in the dark.
At the foot of the bed they settle their sleeves
and exchange valedictory pecks,
then step to the sides, turn down the sheet,
and lie side by side on their backs.

They have long grown accustomed to the hum
of passion at work in the walls,
the bees crawling over swollen combs
to cram every inch with cells,
till the sheer weight of honey unconsumed
shows with the ceiling's fall.

THE DRIVER

Twice we watched him leave us:
once when the car loaded with us died
and rolled to the side of a highway into Nashville
in boiling August; later with cancer.
Empty jug in one hand, he walked away
step by step on a strip of pavement
about as wide as his shoulders,
hot wind of traffic panting on his left.
He would find help. He would attract it. Slowly
the rippling heat from the asphalt dissolved him,
his shrinking back looked like anyone's—
he was gone before it disappeared.
We stood staring anyway
by the highway barrier wall
with mimosa tree-tips reaching over
as the other cars rushed by us
toward their accidents at a hundred miles an hour.

WIND-WHITTLED

We slogged in a sea of wind, sponge divers
free to pick up pennies but never
to shed our brick-foot boots and rise
above the thrashing trees.
The dog was either otter-smooth,
if she faced north,
or fluffed open from behind
like a dandelion.
Litter and leaves scurried sideways near the ground,
or leaped up, yet the sun beamed straight down,
so our legs and arms
could be bare and warm—
though so many molecules streamed stripped from our skin
that dogs statewide caught our scent.
We were diminished by the time we got home
and lurched into the sheltering front room,
whose quiet felt welcome against the ear, yet porous,
once the door was slammed for us.

Where do they go? she asked while washing her hands,
meaning the pipes, mostly, as well as the water and soap
and the stuff that whooshed away with a tug
of the toilet's chain. Her German grandma,
well acquainted with life before indoor plumbing,
gave an answer that sprouted
in the curious granddaughter's mind.
A smart kid, all the aunts said so,
and her pop, sometimes, with a slightly different inflection.
Though too smart now to try digging to China,
she liked the idea of Earth shaped like a marble,
her best blue shooter, snug in the crook of her finger
with her thumb tight ready to spring it
while she cast an acquisitive eye on a solar system
of aggies and immies in a circle of chalk.
The pipes could run from her house to Downers Grove
and Juanita Splitgerber's new house in Carbondale.
They could go all the way to the White House,
to Niagara Falls, and the king of Siam's bathroom.
So with a cheerful vision of a generously connected globe,
she ducked back after supper's discussion
of her mother's favorite, redheaded brother
whose work made him travel too much these days,
and she shouted down the toilet, "Hi, Uncle Calvin!"

SHE TOUCHES MY HAND

Soft hair's-tip touch on the back of my arm
and I smack it too late,
the previous mosquito has found me again,
or her daughter, granddaughter, or seventh cousin,
one and the same to me and though I
know she works automatically to survive,
she radiates witty, malicious cunning—
I feel it as she feels my warmth
and carbon dioxide, the kitchen is full
of our sense of each other,
no wonder I can't get anything done.
She brushes my knuckles
so gently it makes me fierce,
and worse, when at last she crouches on me—
dark double tripod jagged as lightning—
I won't feel it, the contact my skin
keeps imagining now while she hovers elsewhere,
brushes my elbow with her wings—
or her feet? or her mouth, which I tell myself
can't laugh, only pierce, inject, and drink?
She's drawn to me because I drink mango juice
and eat too many strawberries in June,
because of my pomegranate soap and rosemary lotion,
because I draw near the blossom of TV
that flickers like a mosquito's spiel—now I've lost her,
watching my hand, snapping to check my shoulder

while she sips behind my knee. She rises,
a berry full of my blood, singing
that I will itch all summer.

HIS COURTSHIP

With my leaf cloak, with my shoes of lacquered sesame,
I will dazzle the fairy princess.
Firefly paint on my eyes.
With a red feather I'll divert her
from the oversight of her retinue,
and guide her—gently!—amid the grass
to my shining door, flush with the ground.
Introduce her to the black throat behind it,
the seven thousand stairs.
At home she may catch by glowworm's light
a glimpse of my six barbed, crooked legs.
Reproach me for my subterfuge, my forcefulness,
for never using my covered wings to fly,
for never discussing our future.
I am patient.
Shrew or slug or queen bee, she may eat whatever she chooses.
To our children she will be only sweet and tender.

IN ANGANGUEO

She was in Mexico for some paper chain of reasons,
same way she landed anywhere in her days of plenty—
so many languages to pick up, countries to travel through,
mouths to consider kissing, and she could
walk all day, eat anything, add hot sauce,
ask for money from home without reckoning,
wake at noon and stretch without pain.

Then after one ridiculously cold night—
"It's never like this," the guide said—
she stood knee-deep in monarch butterflies
and shivered, once. Not from cold; maybe
from acres of crepe wings stiff in a low breeze,
antennae against her shins.
Little boys in drifts of dulling orange were trying
to pack balls of wings to throw at one another;
she thought perhaps she wouldn't have children.
Or guides, like this one who soothingly repeated,
"The monarchs are sleeping."

STRADIVARIUS SECRETS

The breast must be flexible,
  with a brittle skin;
the neck perfectly straight,
  but curved in cross section;
the body deep and slender,
  made of two trees,
  one evergreen,
  one with fiery grain
  outlined by infection.

Two flat wooden slices
  must be slimmed and trussed,
  taught to bend,
curved to contain
  a singular voice
  between the pine breast
  and maple back,
for which purpose we let the wood soak
  a full nine months
  in sodium, potassium, iron,
  this bacterium, that fungus.

And to seal and make it vibrant,
  let it be candied
in powdered glass, porcelain and amber,
  ox bile, coral, quartz, insecticide,
  powdered ruby and sapphire, chicken blood,

pectin and sugar.
Burnish the outer layer
        of a box of air and dust,
        whispering, *Be like us,*
but *live forever.*

THE CASIMIR EFFECT

Of all the forces that stir and bully matter,
one of the weakest is the Casimir effect:
Say two little silver squares face each other,
a hairbreadth apart. The quantum particles
seething at their backs exert approximately
the pressure of one blood cell within a hand
against the palm. So prodded,
those two tin Scrabble tiles might tend
toward each other, might even hope to touch.

It makes a better story to leave out
the other six billion tiles, the thousands
we lived among, the hundred who knew us
more or less, and our rounded, mismatched shapes.
Like the rest, we were surrounded
by active nothingness, pierced by rays
from distant sources, dark in a cosmos of light,
shielded and impeded by dust, while novas
and black holes conducted stern business
and mercifully the music of the spheres intoned
too low for us to know we heard—

but unlike the rest, you drew near to me and stilled.
Then naturally less chaos lay between us
than roiled behind us or on either side,
and a scarlet dot in a capillary

bumped the heel of my hand, tipping it
minutely forward. We both observed
the Casimir effect. It was feeble at first.

I AM SAINT MADELGAIRE

My name is Madelgaire, and my name is Vincent.
Husband, father, and son-in-law of saints,
I am a saint as well, though simply an abbot
at my death, which took place, so they say,
in six hundred seventy-seven, more or less.
The life purported to be mine
was set down later, in a time starved for miracles—
a patchwork of marvels filched
from stories of more remarkable saints,
such as my wife, Waudru.
Why should this trouble you,
scribe in the twenty-first century?
Did you not know written history
could be mistaken, medieval Christians zealous?
Need you know more of me
than that I founded two monasteries in France,
lived perhaps sixty years, called my children
Landric, Dentelin, Aldetrude,
and Madelberte? It's more than I know of you.
Perhaps it would help to think of me
as one of the many who fall like leaves
to enrich God's garden? No, I thought not.
Write this: Madelgaire was a sinner
who loved his Lord. Not enough?
You may add this safely:
He stubbed his toe. He bit his tongue.

Sore throat, nausea, backache, he made their acquaintance.
His skin puffed in soft pink circles
where insects bit him. Sometimes, although
aware he would worsen the itch, he scratched.

What do you wish to learn?
That I had two eyes, two ears, a nose, a mouth,
four limbs, ten fingers, ten toes, at least to begin with—
what color eyes, how many teeth I kept,
whether I was good to look on,
was there a scar by my lower lip
or above my left knee,
and how did I come to have it?
Suppose I say that at fourteen
I lay braced on my elbows
in a field of plain white flowers
and felt myself fully blessed
without thought of my Lord—
and next morning the flowers were gone.
Next I may tell you that although like you
I consider the multitudes of God's children gone before
and know myself outnumbered,
I do not feel estranged.
And I will give you my blessing, though
this is not my voice, but yours, tricked out
in the flimsy puppet-mitten of my name.

Tell yourself: I was like you.
I was not like you. You will
never know what I did, but may yet
know as much as I.

SHANIDAR, NOW IRAQ

When bones and flesh have finished their business together,
we lay them carefully, in positions they're willing to keep,
and cover them over.
Their eyes and ours won't meet anymore. We hope.

It's one of the oldest rules we mostly follow.
In the deep Stone Age in Shanidar, now Iraq,
someone or all of them laid or threw on the grandfather's chest
whatever was blooming—
Saint-Barnaby's-thistle, yarrow, hollyhock...
His was their only burial before the frost.

For millennia, then, the dead might go under with thistle,
quantities of red ocher, a chunk of meat.
Now we have everlasting bouquets of plastic;
now we have hundreds a day to bag and box and pickle
to recross the Atlantic.

Light a row of oil wells and kneel
on sand too much embroiled for tombs.
Regrettably, something of the smell
is of bodies suddenly buried in fallen stones.
But some is incense, pinches of pulverized Baghdad rising
in ceremonial smoke:
dust of combatants, onlookers, miscellaneous limbs,
contents of hovels, contents of museums,
ancient pollen of yarrow and hollyhock.

RITUAL SANDWICH

Lying on my side in garments of dust,
in the outline of my wooden bier
among animal bones and vessels of painted clay,
I receive you to the ritual meal
the living are bidden to share with the dead—
my first guest in three thousand years and more,
since the Hittites roasted my city and devoured it.
Clean water can be a kingly drink,
and the meat in your hand, I know its aroma,
on which I will dine, while you eat the substance.

Greetings, um, Newly Revealed but Nameless One
Facing East with Legs Bent at the Knees:
I'll chew my sandwich beside your grave
and spill a few drops from my water bottle;
I hope that's how it was done. So the Hittites
consumed your city-state—taking turns
with Assyrians and Egyptians, I guess.
Empires swell and change shape and waste away
like bodies with deadly cancers. Whereas
seven times my body has wholly replaced itself,
cell by cell, since I was born,
but I still have a mole on the back of my neck,
blue eyes, and one crooked toe. Even dead,
we bony creatures do our best
to leave a mark—
if not a mask of beaten gold

or a casket engraved with feathers, perhaps
a richer concentration of fungus,
a patch where grass is younger and thicker,
a sunken place in a field. On a shelf
in my office far away lies an ammonite—
a spiral older even than you—
that once was a living, swimming shell
but turned up in the flank of a desert mountain
with every curve precisely remade in red opal.
Back there we'll blab on paper
of what you teach us about ourselves, but honestly
(I'll whisper, no one can hear us)
I somehow feel sure
that you never gave a thought to our education—
and never reached for our approval
or yearned for our understanding.
I honor you for that.
And thank you for your success anyway in causing
thin air to eddy and drop its sand
to outline and preserve some parts
of you. Cheers, Nameless One.
Drink, as I turn mutton and bread
and olives into myself.

They lived here almost fifty years,
by a stream of clear water, in a well-built house of stone.
Hervenard kept two hundred sheep in the valley
with a dog that was part wolf; Isenhedda
tended her garden, spun wool and wove it, singing.
She bore three girls, one with a beautiful face,
and combed their hair with her mother-of-pearl comb, singing,
and one son, who went to war and came back late
with one arm and a sack of gold.
They had a few bad years of fevers and acorn flour,
but mostly good cheer, mutton and apples,
her songs about the swan or the oak tree,
his tales of long ago and far away.

—

They lived here almost fifty years,
by a   well-built house of stone.
Herven   kept two hundred sheep
with a   part wolf; Isenhedda
tended her   wool and wove it
She bore three girls   with   beautiful
                        hair with her   pearl comb, singing,
and one son, who went to war
with one arm and a sack of gold.
They had   years of fevers and acorn flour,
          good cheer   and apples,
                  the swan or the oak tree,
      tales of long ago and far away.

They lived here
by a   well   of stone.
He   kept two   sheep
with a   wolf; s   he
tended her

                                beautiful
                hair with her   pearl comb,
        one son
with one arm   of gold.
They had   ears of   corn
            d   eer   and apples,
            the swan   tree,
        long ago

        ⌐

They lived
by a   stone

with a   wolf;   he
tended her
                                    beautiful   hair
                with her   comb

                of gold.

                                            apple
                                        tree,
            long ago

They lived

long ago

long ago

LAST WILL

1

Know all by these presents that I the undersigned,
being of sound mind, bad belly, and crumbling infrastructure,
do hereby distribute my dubious treasures as follows:

The papers in my filing cabinets, and stacked on the shelves by
    the desk,
and piled on the desk, and on the chairs,
and on the study floor, I leave to you, paper wasps.
You won't have to scrape my windowsill any longer
for paltry helpings of cellulose. Chew
decades of pages down to nested hexagons
of symmetry and spit, so the ink at last
forms satisfactory patterns.

The books on the other shelves in the study,
in the bedrooms, kitchen, living room, and attic,
under the tables, beside the bed, on the washing machine,
behind the doors, on the dressers,
and boxed above the water heater,
I leave to you, dainty silverfish,
and you, generations of mold and mildew.
I fended you off as long as I could,
yet you've never borrowed a book and failed to return it,
never poured contempt on my favorites,
never used *lay* for *lie*. Here,
fall to, have them, cover to cover.

My jewelry—beads and chains and one true diamond—
and baubles such as the silver llama, glass elephant,
and pansy cup, the marbles and smooth stones,
I leave to you, bowerbirds. Choose what you wish
for your fantasy castles, designed to attract
the most appreciative mates. But don't dither too long
or the crows, the shrunken dragons of our time,
will beat you to it and refuse to share.

The toys, gimcracks, and souvenirs,
from the tin windmill to Phineas the rubber poodle—
individual delights, but together
a prickly haystack oppressive to the spirit—
they should be heaped in an old red wagon
and trundled all over town.
Let the trundler sow them along the sidewalks
without looking back.

2

To the calcium and salts of my bone and nerve cells,
thanks I suppose are in order, though I won't miss
the five kinds of back pain they did so well.
I release them to do something easier—
be seashells, perhaps. Or the sea.

As for the sparks in my fingers, brain stem,
untied cardiac shoestrings—they have to go somewhere.
Don't they? Into a paramecium's twirl,
a little kind heat on someone's skin?
A violet would be sappy, the glow of a bobtail squid...
wait. This part isn't up to me, is it?
None of it is. Perhaps I should practice:
Take what you like, whoever you are,
and do with it what you please.
I won't say a word.

NOTES

IPHIGENIA IN AULIS (PAGE 9)

The "four ascending notes" are from the overture of Gluck's *Iphigénie en Aulide*.

HOLLOW BOOM SOFT CHIME: THE THAI ELEPHANT ORCHESTRA (PAGE 23)

Elephant musicians live at the Thai Elephant Conservation Center in Lampang, Thailand, and have recorded three CDs.

SPEAKING OF THE OCTOPUS (PAGE 44)

Forty thousand three hundred twenty (40,320) is the factorial of eight: $8 \times 7 \times 6 \times 5 \times 4 \times 3 \times 2 \times 1$.

IF GOD MADE JAM (PAGE 77)

From *A Short Catechism for Young Children:*

Q. Why ought you to serve God?
A. Because he made, preserves, and redeemed me.

AUNT LYDIA CONTEMPLATES LIFE, ART, AND PETRI DISHES (PAGE 81)

A pair of astronomers concluded in 2001 that the average color of the universe was a "shade of pale turquoise." A year later they changed their verdict, somewhat disappointingly, to beige.

Sarah Lindsay, recipient of a Lannan Literary Fellowship, is the author of *Twigs & Knucklebones* (Copper Canyon Press, 2008). Previously she published two chapbooks, *Bodies of Water* (1986) and *Insomniac's Lullaby* (1989), and two books in the Grove Press Poetry Series: *Primate Behavior* (1997), a finalist for the National Book Award, and *Mount Clutter* (2002). Her work has also appeared in *The Best American Poetry, The Georgia Review, McSweeney's, The New York Times, The Paris Review, Parnassus, Poetry, Reader's Digest, The 2011 Rhysling Anthology: The Best Science Fiction, Fantasy and Horror Poetry of 2010,* and other publications, and has been awarded the J. Howard and Barbara M.J. Wood Prize and a Pushcart Prize.

A native of Cedar Rapids, Iowa, Lindsay graduated from St. Olaf College with a B.A. and a Paracollege major in English and creative writing. She holds an M.F.A. in creative writing from the University of North Carolina–Greensboro. She has worked at Coe College as a typist, at the Cedar Rapids *Gazette* in the makeup department, and at Unicorn Press as a typesetter, printer, bookbinder, and floor-sweeper. She now earns her keep as a copy editor at Pace in Greensboro, North Carolina.

Lannan Literary Selections

For two decades Lannan Foundation has supported the publication
and distribution of exceptional literary works. Copper Canyon Press
gratefully acknowledges their support.

LANNAN LITERARY SELECTIONS 2013

Kerry James Evans, *Bangalore*

Sarah Lindsay, *Debt to the Bone-Eating Snotflower*

Lisa Olstein, *Little Stranger*

Roger Reeves, *King Me*

Ed Skoog, *Rough Day*

RECENT LANNAN LITERARY SELECTIONS FROM
COPPER CANYON PRESS

James Arthur, *Charms Against Lightning*

Natalie Diaz, *When My Brother Was an Aztec*

Matthew Dickman and Michael Dickman, *50 American Plays*

Michael Dickman, *Flies*

Laura Kasischke, *Space, in Chains*

Deborah Landau, *The Last Usable Hour*

Michael McGriff, *Home Burial*

Heather McHugh, *Upgraded to Serious*

Valzhyna Mort, *Collected Body*

Lucia Perillo, *Inseminating the Elephant*

John Taggart, *Is Music: Selected Poems*

Tung-Hui Hu, *Greenhouses, Lighthouses*

Jean Valentine, *Break the Glass*

C.D. Wright, *One Big Self: An Investigation*

Dean Young, *Fall Higher*

For a complete list of Lannan Literary Selections from
Copper Canyon Press, please search "Lannan" on our website:
www.coppercanyonpress.org

Poetry is vital to language and living. Since 1972, Copper Canyon Press has published extraordinary poetry from around the world to engage the imaginations and intellects of readers, writers, booksellers, librarians, teachers, students, and donors.

WE ARE GRATEFUL FOR THE MAJOR SUPPORT PROVIDED BY:

THE PAUL G. ALLEN
FAMILY FOUNDATION

Lannan

THE MAURER FAMILY
FOUNDATION

NATIONAL
ENDOWMENT
FOR THE ARTS

 WASHINGTON STATE
ARTS COMMISSION

Anonymous

Arcadia Fund

John Branch

Diana and Jay Broze

Beroz Ferrell & The Point, LLC

Mimi Gardner Gates

Gull Industries, Inc.
on behalf of William and Ruth True

Mark Hamilton and Suzie Rapp

Carolyn and Robert Hedin

Steven Myron Holl

Lakeside Industries, Inc.
on behalf of Jeanne Marie Lee

Maureen Lee and Mark Busto

Brice Marden

New Mexico Community Foundation

H. Stewart Parker

Penny and Jerry Peabody

Joseph C. Roberts

Cynthia Lovelace Sears and Frank Buxton

The Seattle Foundation

Dan Waggoner

Charles and Barbara Wright

The dedicated interns and faithful
volunteers of Copper Canyon Press

To learn more about underwriting Copper Canyon Press titles,
please call 360-385-4925 ext. 103

The Chinese character for poetry is made up of two parts: "word" and "temple." It also serves as pressmark for Copper Canyon Press.

The text is set in Baskerville 10 with titles set in Monotype Bulmer. Both are digital reworkings of eighteenth-century English typefaces. Book design and composition by VJB/Scribe.